You Haven't Lived Here If You Haven't...

northwestern pennsylvania

Compiled by Robb Frederick

Published by

Erie Times·News

Times Publishing Company
Erie, Pennsylvania

Printed by
Pediment Publishing
A Division of The Pediment Group, Inc.

Foreword

I was an odd fit for "You Haven't Lived Here if You Haven't …," a column that appears every Monday in the Erie Times-News.

I hadn't lived here, except for a stretch in college. I had never chucked a puck at center ice during the break at an Otters game. I had not walked the top of the Union City Dam. I hadn't tried the bumbleberry pie at the Academy Diner, where the owner, Lynn Kowalski, set plates on her grandmother's old Formica-topped table.

I have now.

I love Erie because of this book — because of Ross Peters, a retired welder who populated his lawn with chicken-wire dinosaurs, and because of the cross on "The Pantocrator," the great mosaic in the stairway at Gannon University. I love what makes us different: the bocce games at Bobby's Place, the fish at the Linesville spillway, the scoops of Blue Moon at Dari Creem.

Too much of the world looks the same these days. There are 136 Wal-Marts in Guatemala. There are 580 McDonald's arches in China.

There is just one statue of George Washington in a British uniform, and that's in Waterford.

You haven't really lived here until you've rubbed his toe for luck.

Robb Frederick
Project Director

Cover Photo

The road-sign flowers on Route 322 are always in bloom. The art project covers a 1,200-foot stretch of a PennDOT fence, with flowers, a singing cowboy and a spinning Ferris wheel, all cut from old road signs. "It's fueling a kind of optimism that we can change our community, that we can make it better," said Amara Geffen, the art professor at Allegheny College who coordinates the project.

Acknowledgements

You Haven't Lived Here If You Haven't...

Project Staff

Project Director	Robb Frederick
Assistant Project Director/Promotions	Lisa Shade
Series Editors	Jeffrey Hileman
	Doug Oathout
Marketing/Promotions	Kate Breese, Intern
Art Director	Karen Burchill
Design Production/Cover	Jill Chaklos
Photographers	Lauren M. Anderson
	John Bartlett
	Janet B. Campbell
	Rob Engelhardt
	Rich Forsgren
	Jack Hanrahan
	Vivian Johnson
	Zach Long
	Jim Martin
	Christopher Millette
	Jimmie Presley
	Greg Wohlford

Contents

You Haven't Lived Here If You Haven't...

11 Dominick's 24 Hour Eatery

13 Presque Isle State Park

15 Erie Otters

17 Conneaut Lake Park

19 Ross Peters' T. Rex

21 Freeport Restaurant

23 Erie Zoo

25 Hearthside Rest Pet Cemetery

27 Albion Carousel

29 Erie SeaWolves

31 Linesville Spillway

33 Smith Provision Co.

35 Louis W. Bierbauer

37 St. Patrick Catholic Church

39 Barracks Beach Yoga

41 Allegheny College

43 Sara's

45 Cathedral Prep vs. McDowell

47 Warner Theatre

49 Joseph C. Martin Golf Club

51 Denny's Ice Cream Stand

53 Bobby's Place

55 Canadohta Lake

57 Gannon University

59 Panama Rocks

61 Fuhrman's Cider Mill & Bakery

63 Edinboro University of Pennsylvania

65 Books Galore

67 Millcreek Mall

69 Erie Maennerchor Club

71 The Athenaeum Hotel

73 Ice Wine

75 Mercyhurst College

77 Waldameer Park & Water World

79 Route 322 Road-sign Art

81 Fiesler's Gas Station

83 Goodell Gardens

85 Hank's Frozen Custard

87 Dick Schaefer's Car Art

89 West Erie Plaza

91 Pithole Visitor Center

93 Sigsbee Reservoir

95 Presque Isle BMX

97 Mason Farms Country Market

99 Union Station

101 Burton Park

103 The U.S. Brig Niagara

105 Boston Store

107 Erie Cemetery

109 Bicentennial Tower

... sobered up with a meatball omelet at Dominick's.

It's not the most obvious combo: hand-rolled meatballs stuffed in a pocket of egg, provolone and 12-hour sauce, stirred by the cook Nicky's kid sold with the kitchen.

But it does serve a purpose.

"You come in here knowing it's going to sober you up," says the owner, Bill Rieger, a fitness buff with a soft spot for the $2.49 breakfast special. "It's made my business what it is."

What it is is tradition: A smoky, late-night oasis where the coffee's hot and the booths are chopped from countertops, and where photos of the old owner, Nick Fedei, and his favorite waitress, Geraldine "Sissy" Angelotti, still hang on the wall, looking on, never minding when the night drags on a little longer.

The meatball omelet
Dominick's 24 Hour Eatery, 123 E. 12th St.

... paddled through the lagoons at Presque Isle State Park.

It's different, down low to the water, in a kayak brushing back spatterdock lily pads.

"It's like riding on top of a giant aquarium," says Jeremy Rekich, a park naturalist who leads paddle classes.

It's a full one, too. Since 1936, when the state cut a channel 15 feet deep, making new room for water-skiers, Mother Nature has crept back, adding bulrush, button bush and purple-leafed pickerel weed. There are deer, beavers and great blue herons; kingfishers, spotted gars and the occasional big-winged osprey. And there's not a bicycle in sight.

"You get a whole new perspective out here on a boat," Rekich says. "You're kind of earning it."

Presque Isle State Park Lagoons
Long Pond and beyond. Kayak and canoe rentals are run from the Presque Isle Boat Livery.

... chucked a puck at center ice during the break at an Otters game.

At the buzzer - about when the Mississauga IceDogs do the bone toss and the Ottawa 67's do the baby race - the arena staff sets out nine trash cans and a tiny orange bucket.

The announcer cues the crowd, and foam pucks rain down, flung at the bucket, for a cash prize as high as $500, and at the trash cans, for a shot at lift tickets, movie passes and a month of free cable.

"It's like the half-court shot in basketball," says Angela Matusiak, who hands out the prizes. "You just close your eyes, throw it and pray."

The numbered pucks bounce and roll and weeble their way across the ice, and you see the genius in this: a 30-second spectacle that still leaves time for the beer line.

Chuck-A-Puck
Take your shot during the second intermission of any home Otters game.

... screamed from the back seat of the Blue Streak.

The old wooden coaster is a shallow-track out-and-back, an Ed Vettel design that is the last of its kind.

The passenger train dates to 1937, when the coaster opened. It bumps through the tunnel, tugs up the first steep hill and levels off for one nervous, what's-next second. Then it looses you to two minutes of jostling, jaw-knocking, bunny-hop drops.

There are no loops, no tubular-steel tracks and no fancy magnetic brake fins - just the lurch of that old-fashioned lift chain, clack-clack-clacking till there's no going back. And that's all that matters.

It's true that Conneaut Lake Park has faded, and the Blue Streak could use some paint, but the point of the day hasn't changed: On this ride, you know you're alive.

The Blue Streak
Conneaut Lake Park. The coaster, which hits top speed at 46 mph, is the sixth-oldest in the United States. The original color was yellow.

... posed for a photo with Ross Peters' 12-foot T. rex.

It's kitsch, but it's a hit with the kids. They look past the rebar and chicken wire, the concrete and house paint, and they see the real deal.

There's an elephant, too. You can climb into that one, if you don't mind the wasps. But few do.

"The kids get out of the car and run right past that elephant, like it isn't even there," says Peters, a retired welder who made a concrete whale for the Erie Zoo. (It broke when workers tried to move it.) "They go right for that dinosaur."

The T. rex has a baby now, a mini Jurassic lawn jockey that's just right for climbing. Peters can see it from his neat yellow house. He'll stand there sometimes, when a car parks, a child runs out and a dad reaches for the camera. He'll smile a minute, thinking, 'Yeah, retirement's all right."

Ross Peters' lawn sculptures
On the 700 block of Bartlett Road in Harborcreek, down the street from Shades Beach.

... tried a fried dill pickle at the Freeport Restaurant.

Fat America will fry anything: eggplant, okra, chicken, even Snickers bars.

The pickle tradition started in the South, at an Arkansas drive-in called the Duchess. The owner, Bernell Austin, served beer-battered spears to workers across the street, at the Atkins Pickle Plant.

His gimmick caught on. It spread to other menus, and it caught the fancy of an old cook at the Freeport, which opened in 1976, after stints as a home, a deer-processing shop and a corner gas pump. The restaurant is known for its smokehouse, but it's the pickles, chipped and crispy, with a side of ranch for dipping, that put the salt on soul food.

People say Elvis loved the stuff. And that's enough for us.

The Freeport Restaurant
At the intersection of Routes 5 and 89, North East. The long beam above the bar washed out of the lake and onto the property of the owners, Jerry and Judy Holdsworth.

... looped the zoo with Engineer Dewey.

He drives the Safariland Express, a scale version of the C.P. Huntington, the Civil War train that carried track for the Transcontinental Railroad.

He'll ring the bell - unless there are wallaby babies nearby - and take you over the trestle and into the tunnel, where a black-lit bear waits in paint.

On the second trestle, at the not-quite-frightening height of 20 feet, 3 and ¾ inches, he'll say something about the "thundering rapids of mighty Mill Creek." And in the open area, where the fallow deer and Egyptian geese move free, he'll still that four-cylinder Ford engine until Betsy, the buffalo, decides to step off the track.

It's a reminder, for Dewey, Dwayne and the other engineers, of who really lives here.

The Safariland Express
At the Erie Zoo. Be sure to listen to the engineer's script, some of which goes back to 1965, when GE volunteers laid the track.

... gone to Bonzo's grave.

Walk to the center of Hearthside Rest Pet Cemetery, past Stinky Clark, Chippie Lesko, CheWee Ramos and Itty Bit Saurborn, and you'll spot Bonzo, the film star. He played off Ronald Reagan in the 1951 chimp comedy "Bedtime for Bonzo."

Years later, he was sold to a circus. He got sick on a trip to Buffalo, N.Y., and the whole convoy stopped.

Art Paavola, the doctor at Erie Animal Hospital, couldn't do much for him; chimps were not a normal part of his dog-and-farm practice. Before long, Bonzo was dead. And Paavola, who had a brand-new animal cemetery - nine shaded acres off Rick Road - offered a spot to the circus man.

Bonzo is still out there, surrounded by dogs, cats and an iguana with a 3-foot tail. "He made us laugh," the stone reads. But it must have been more than that: Someone keeps bringing flowers.

Hearthside Rest Pet Cemetery
Rick Road, off Sterrettania Road. The current owner, Tom Paavola, added a scavenged fire hydrant, a bit of whimsy at the plot for his dog, Beemer.

... ridden the Albion carousel.

The Lions Club bought it in 1947, after a local child was turned away from a traveling carnival ride.

For years it was free. The borough even sent school buses to bring the country kids in for rides.

The carousel, in its little white building, with the windows raised up like the front of a county fair food booth, embodies the pitch-in spirit of another time. The engine mechanism was built by a borough employee who took parts from his wife's vacuum. The horses, which have stood mid-leap since at least 1886, have authentic hair tails dyed by Geri Dean and her friends.

Dean starts the ride, pushing hard with her shoulder. "When I get that old," she says, laughing, "someone's going to have to give me a push, too."

The Albion carousel
Albion Borough Park. Rides cost 50 cents.

... spent extra at Buck Night.

It's the most proletariat of promotions: A SeaWolves ticket for the same price as the popcorn, the beer and the Smith's hot dog.

Add the crack of the bat, a birthday on the scoreboard and "Ascend to Charge" on the organ, and you've got small-town ball at its best.

The team tried its first Buck Night in 1999. The crowds came out, the beer got them loud, and the players felt the force of a rollicking full house.

A Buck Night can bring Jerry Uht Park to a standing-room capacity of close to 7,000 fans. They've emptied as many as 110 kegs, which comes to roughly 16,500 cups of beer, which is almost enough to make us love a Monday in the summer.

Buck Night
Monday nights at Jerry Uht Park. Blame inflation: Tickets now cost $3.

... fed stale bread to the fish at the Linesville Spillway.

The upper 2,500 acres of Pymatuning Reservoir drain here, and that draws carp.

They roil the water, their mouths suckering, their tails slapping, their bodies so close the ducks actually walk on their backs.

The novelty of that draws nearly 350,000 people each year.

State officials have started $2 million in improvements to the spillway facilities. But the experience is still as simple as it was in the 1940s, when the first small crowds tossed pinches of week-old Wonder bread and watched the water erupt.

Linesville Spillway
Part of Pymatuning State Park. Follow signs from Route 6 in Linesville, Crawford County.

... heard the pop of a Smith's hot dog.

Bite into the thin skin casing and you taste summer at the speedway, or the sun on Jerry Uht Park.

A Smith's isn't as red as a down-south foot-long, or as garlicky as a New York City cart dog. It isn't as salty as the ones Anton Weber made when he bought the business in 1949, after he married and asked his boss for a small raise, only to see his pay cut by half when the man knew how much he needed the work.

Still, the company sells nearly 2 million pounds every year. The lean, beefy flavor is a favorite of NASCAR driver Mark Martin, who sometimes lets fans into the pits if they bring them. Rush drummer Neil Peart likes them enough to keep an order on his tour contract, Smith's President Mike Weber says.

"Our customers are as loyal as any," Weber says. "But they like the product the way is. They get nervous if we even try to change the label."

Smith Provision Co.
Smith's has shipped as far as Uzbekistan, as a favor to the Army's 542nd Quartermaster Co.

... traced a name back to Louie Bierbauer.

The second baseman hit .306 for the Brooklyn Wonders, the Players' League team, in 1890, a year after he quit the Philadelphia Athletics.

The next year, when the union teams split, he defected to the National League, signing with the last-place Pittsburgh Alleghenies. They played at Recreation Park, with the catcher's pet monkey buried under home plate.

Bierbauer had a rough year there, but he bounced back, and his impact is still on the cap. Philadelphia fans, angry that he left the Athletics, pressed the American Association, which argued that "the action of the Pittsburgh club in signing Bierbauer was piratical."

Today, Pirates fans celebrate that contract grab with pennants, toy bats and foam fingers. And most don't even know it.

Louis W. Bierbauer
The low-cut stone over his grave in Erie Cemetery celebrates a legacy outside baseball, calling him, simply, "Father."

... walked the Stations of the Cross at St. Patrick Catholic Church.

Catholics who pray the stations pay tribute to the sacrifice of Christ.

At St. Patrick, where the Stations are life-size, cut from 1,000-pound blocks of German fir, the experience is stirring.

The hand-carved figures have been fully restored. The colors - rusts, umbers, indigos and gold leaf, and eyes the color of a clear June sky - add to the immediacy of the raised whip, the weeping mother and the spike pounded through an open palm.

Here, the story of Christ's passion, told on so many Sundays in so many cities, rises above the symbols and enfolds the soul.

St. Patrick Catholic Church
130 E. Fourth St.

... held the cobra pose during sunset yoga at Barracks Beach.

The teacher, Michael Plasha, tuned in when the Beatles met the Maharishi.

His prompts come dubbed with an Om.

"We're looking for the 'ding,'" he says, directing the next stretch.

He means the optimal feeling of a mind and body moved properly. "Where you feel it is where you need it," he says.

He slowly goes through the motions: the locust, the cobra and the downward-facing dog; the diamond, which helps with digestion; the bound-angle, which can ease PMS; and half a dozen others, until the class is standing, raising their hands, appreciating the wind and the sun and the lap of the lake water, their backs tingling, their toes wiggling, their souls singing:

Ding.

... bobbed an echo off the Allegheny College quad sculpture.

There's a sweet spot in the center of "Presence of Seven in the Light of Movement," the glass campus Stonehenge, a ring of iridescent wafer plates shish-kebabbed on steel rods. Anything you say there smacks the glass and bounces back, back, back.

That wasn't planned. The sculpture, installed in the fall of 2002, assembled in two weeks from 2,700 pieces, was meant to be seen. The tallest of the seven figures rises 17 feet. The lowest, a glass wedge as long as a Mazda Miata, cuts right through a bench.

Sculpted by the London artist Danny Lane, whose "Borealis" was built into the design of the General Motors headquarters, it's a calming wall of glowing green glass. Then the clouds move, the colors erupt, and the sculpture becomes a 100,000-pound prism, different every time you visit.

"Presence of Seven in the Light of Movement"
Senior Circle, Allegheny College. Ronald Harrell, a campus mathematician, designed the jigs that gave the glass layers their shape.

.... stood "15 back" at Sara's.

That's a kitchen yell, code for the crowd at the counter, which sits on the right side of a 1950s Crown Vic.

The line is a sign that Sean Candela is doing it right. On his first day, back in 1980, he made maybe $20. But he built the little restaurant into a peninsula tradition, a burger joint with bottled Cokes and a Phillips 66 sign by the drive-through.

"We're fortunate to be associated with summer," he says. But he misses it. He's busy in the kitchen, doing business in his paper hat and his Howdy Doody shirt button. He'll work 180 days straight, not stopping until Sept. 30.

The winters are his, with time for the kids and a tradition far from the kitchen: Cleveland Browns season tickets.

Sara's

25 Peninsula Drive, Erie. Candela named the restaurant for his mother, Sara Coyne. She worked the peat bogs in Ireland, took double-decker bus fares during the blitzkrieg of London and was a longtime carhop at the Home Drive-In.

... picked a side in the Cathedral Prep-McDowell rivalry.

Some say it started with Sister Cornelia, a stickler for English who kept her Prep class late, delaying the teams' first meeting back in 1930.

Others say it's simpler than that. "We're the two best teams," says Tom Jakubowski, the athletic director at McDowell. "We're the last two bullies on the block."

For a while, the fans took it too far. They tagged the orange Prep bus with the Trojans' blue hue. They burned a big "P" on the McDowell field. They spray-painted "McDowell" - misspelled - on the Prep sidewalk. And then, in 1977, they threw eggs at St. Peter Cathedral.

"There was a rumble, right out of 'West Side Story,'" says the Rev. John Detisch, who heads the Prep alumni association.

Now they keep the fight to Friday nights, under the lights. The teams hit a little harder, run a little faster and find whatever it takes to make every snap matter.

... imagined the black-tie grandeur of the Warner Theatre.

It isn't difficult. Except for the seats - which, until the orchestra pit is fixed, start with Row B - the gilded theater, with its gold-backed mirrors, Italian fabrics and Czech glass chandeliers, still looks as it did on opening night, when the marquee blazed under 8,000 lights.

Construction of the Warner cost $1.5 million, and the Depression didn't dent it. The 2,250-seat hall was a Vaudeville draw. Bob Hope told jokes, using a barrel for a chair. Bob Dylan played there. So did Johnny Cash, Dave Matthews and Nat King Cole.

But the Warner, for all its glory, was built for the movies, back when hats mattered and theaters, even with the lights on, were magic.

The Warner Theatre
811 State St., Erie. The best of the second set of seats are still used at the Director's Circle Theatre, in the Renaissance Centre.

... shanked a tee shot at the Joseph C. Martin Golf Club.

Animal handlers at the Erie Zoo find a dozen balls in the bison and goat enclosures every day. They consider it a cost of being so close to a city-owned course that caters to kids.

The nine-hole Martin club, named for a former city councilman and mayor, is a good introduction to the game: an open course, close to several schools, with $9 green fees and a great run of par-threes, each 175 yards or longer.

"Green patrols" walk the course every two days, fixing divots. Club manager Jack Tufts pays them in candy.

His club, plain as it is, moves the sport forward, grooming Tigers who can two-putt and take the place of today's players.

Joseph C. Martin Golf Club
652 Shunpike Road. Bags rent for $4 a round. Pull carts are $1.

... spooned a scoop of Blue Moon.

It smells like Froot Loops. It looks like a soft-serve snowballed Smurf. It's rumored to encourage birth, though it didn't work for Dave Stuck and his wife, who delivered several days late.

"To be honest with you," says Stuck, the manager of Denny's Ice Cream Stand, where they've scooped Blue Moon since 1982, "I'm not a big fan. It's not something I'd ever order. But it flies out of here."

He'll sell 20 gallons on a hot day, but he still can't explain the taste: A hint of raspberry, or almond, or cotton candy with almonds, with the finish of a 1950s Blue Tail Fly cocktail, which mixed Blue Curacao and White Crème de Cacao.

To us, it tastes like a daydream - the "Ollie Ollie Oxen Free!" that summer used to be.

Blue moon ice cream
At Denny's Ice Cream Stand, 929 Parade St., and at Dari Creem, 715 Parade St.

... plinked the pallino in a bocce game at Bobby's Place.

The bar started as a corner grocery. When Bobby Marasco bought it, he knocked down the houses out back. He cut wood borders for three 75-foot bocce courts, and he filled them with raked clay. He hung a chalkboard for the scores.

The Tuesday league teams are on there: House of Usher, Arnone's and the Crow's Nest, the father-son Mozzocco rollers, who drive from Ashtabula, Ohio. "Once you play on a court, you'll never go back to the back yard," Larry Mozzocco says during warm-ups.

The men bend like bowlers, chucking fast-pitch, cloud-spit grounders. The balls clack. The other teams roll back.

"It's the camaraderie," says Tony Pasanen, who comes with his son, Junior.

His proof? The losers buy the food.

Bocce at Bobby's Place
1202 W. 18th St., at the corner of Cranberry. Open courts Thursdays and Saturdays, until the leagues end in September.

... splashed into Canadohta Lake.

The best way is off the roof of the Frog Pond, the restaurant Chuck Lipchik bought in 1978. He had come to Canadohta to buy a Cadillac, a 1957 Eldorado Biarritz. He got it for $800.

The real estate agent stayed on him, and soon he had the restaurant, too. He cut up a yacht and made it the bar. He put in some fish tanks. He built a rooftop water slide, with a tube 6-feet wide.

It's 12 seconds top-to-bottom. It's 263 feet of twisty Louisiana fiberglass, splashed with 2,500 gallons a minute.

"It'll wake you up," Lipchik says.

The line is short. Lipchik has competition now. He's lost out to the big slides and the programmed climate at Splash Lagoon. His slide is kind of like a drive-in now. It's a novelty, a reminder of a time when we still played outside.

The Frog Pond
35765 Circuit Drive, Canadohta Lake.

... looked up at the "Pantocrator."

The stone-and-glass mosaic was inspired by El Greco, and by the Christ icon in the Hagia Sophia, the great church in Constantinople. It was sketched in Germany, on the floor of the Franz Mayer Studio, by the Rev. Peter William Gray, the first artist-in-residence at Gannon University.

Italian craftsmen chopped the glass by hand. For the nose and forehead, they used onyx from Pakistan; for the cheeks, rose marble from Venice.

The Coptic cross, a symbol of the African church, is gold leaf laid on hot glass, melted over in squares that shimmer in open light.

For Gray, the fractured design gave the piece meaning. It suggests, in a way no mural can, that Christ became whole only after he was broken.

The "Pantocrator"

A.J. Palumbo Academic Center, Gannon University. A classic Byzantine mosaic, with black, orange, olive and marbled blues. It has anchored an open stairwell since 1996.

... walked Panama Rocks.

There's a carpet of moss on the top - a soft, damp mat that edges the mile-long path. There are leafy beech and cherry trees. There's a sapsucker tapping at the bark of a century hemlock.

It's a storybook wood, just the sort for Robin Hood, who would have felt some kinship with the outlaws and counterfeiters who once hid loot in the park's black crevasses.

The rocks are spectacular. Big, tilted boulders lean over tabletops of Paleozoic outcrop. Wide shelves of flat rock jut out, opening mazes of narrow, mineshaft passages. The kids venture in, chasing echoes.

An earthquake made this. An Ice Age glacier notched it, leaving cliffs of rock. But it's the trees that keep it interesting. Their long, clawed roots finger out, across slick rock and onto impossible edges. They hold, somehow. They'll own those rocks long after we are gone.

Panama Rocks
Panama, N.Y. Open through Oct. 21.

... tasted Fuhrman's apple cider.

The family-run mill has pressed Cortlands and Ida reds since 1896.

Today they bottle eight gallons a minute. The apples roll out of big wooden bins, down a belt and through a washer - "A bath and two showers," co-owner George Engesser says - before they're chopped in a 10-knife grinder. The sauce that comes out is seedy, with skins; it's pressed against a steel plate until the juice spills over.

Cider is tart when the season starts. At Fuhrman's, that's the Saturday after Labor Day.

In the spring, Engesser goes back to his other job, working heavy machinery with a road crew. The waste product of all those apples - a pasty mash that looks a lot like wet cardboard - goes back to the orchards as mulch. It's a head start on a season that feels a long way off.

Fuhrman's Cider Mill & Bakery
1218 E. Gore Road.

... tried to find Einstein on the ceiling of the Louis C. Cole Auditorium.

The five-panel mural features more than 150 authors, philosophers, explorers, poets and popes, spaced like constellations above the 800 theater seats.

Painted by Alfred James Tulk, a Briton whose religious triptychs were used for World War II battlefield church services, the mural tempts the theater's less-attentive.

"Someone is always looking up," says Tim Cordell, a trumpet player and professor of music history who performs often in the hall. "I do it, too. I've been here 29 years, and I'm still fascinated by it."

It's an abridged history - Jesus, Keats, Caesar and St. Peter; Mozart, Karl Marx, Darwin and Thoth, the Egyptian moon god - limited, with apologies to Einstein, by the size of the room.

Louis C. Cole Auditorium and Memorial Hall
Edinboro University of Pennsylvania. Tulk was called back to "fix" the spelling of Monteverdi. He did, even though he'd had it right the first time.

... shopped for comics at Books Galore.

These aren't the BAM! POW! ZAP! serials of the past, underwritten by sea-monkey ads.

They're paper worlds with shadow, nuance and impossible abs; with soap-opera story lines and strong, flawed heroes who dish out Technicolor deaths.

The moral compass is off. The art bleeds like a Thorazine dream.

"The stories draw you in," says Jeff Phillips, whose mother, Marge, has run the shop since 1985, when she brought another son in for a comic. "It's an escape."

And now it's a Hollywood shortcut. Batman and the Fantastic Four are sure money on the big screen. But true collectors, who keep their comics on cardboard - better to guard against dog-ears - find they're just like readers of Michael Ondaatje, who gave us "The English Patient": They like the books better.

Books Galore
5546 Peach St. More than 250,000 comics in stock, including some 10-cent "X-Men" under the counter.

... realized the Millcreek Mall is shaped like a gun.

The image is clear on the "You Are Here" maps: Sears is the grip, Burlington the rear sight and J.C. Penny, pointed straight at the city, where legend has it the mob wanted the mall built, is the muzzle.

There's no truth to that story, of course. "It's an urban legend," says Matt Boarts, the mall's marketing director, a man clearly not comfortable with talk that links shopping malls and firearms. "I am sure that when the mall was built that was not a consideration."

The truth is a bit more boring: The mall opened in stages, starting with Sears in 1974. Now the available space dictates its shape.

The original mall is ringed with a marble field of free-standing restaurants, bridal shops and dollar cinemas. Add Santa and a Starbucks, and your Christmas gift budget - Mafia or not - is shot.

... hit the duckpins at the Erie Maennerchor Club.

The lanes are in the basement. The pins are little, fitted with rubber collars that muffle the jackpot clatter of a 10-pin game. The collars give the pins play, which is bowler-speak for that lucky bounce that knocks the spare down.

"You do see some strange things," says Jim Grande, a retired school counselor who plays on one of the club's 16 league teams.

The ball is smaller. Most are just 4 pounds, with no finger holes. It's like bowling a bocce ball at a Coors bottle - starting from the far end of your neighbor's driveway.

There's tradition in this. Legend says the sport started in Baltimore, in a bowling alley owned by baseball Hall-of-Famer John "Muggsy" McGraw. He hunted ducks, and when he saw those cut pins scatter, back in 1927, he muttered that it looked like a flock of shot birds. Bowlers have been rolling for them ever since.

Duckpin bowling
For nights a week at the Erie Maennerchor Club, 1607 State St.

... sat in a ladder-back chair at Chautauqua's Athenaeum Hotel.

The 1881 Belle Epoque Victorian resort is large for Chautauqua, where cars are frowned upon and houses are little more than an excuse for a porch.

But it holds quite a bit of history. Amelia Earhart slept there, having landed her plane on the Institution's golf course. Henry Ford and Harvey Firestone dined there, invited by Thomas Edison, whose father-in-law co-founded the Chautauqua community.

Tradition still holds court at the hotel. Guests pay on the American Plan, which includes with the room three meals a day. Dinner comes in five courses.

There is opera in the parlor, which is fitted with white wicker. There is character to the 160 rooms, which are papered with 80 different patterns. But it's the high-columned porch that holds the essence of this old hotel. There may be no better place to waste a late-summer day.

The Athenaeum Hotel
At the Chautauqua Institution, Chautauqua, N.Y.

... tried ice wine.

The difference is in the Brix, which measures the density of sugar in a solution. An average Vidal Blanc will land between 19 and 21 on the Brix scale, which was named for a 19th Century German chemist. An ice wine can go to 37 or 40.

That means it's sweet. "You don't drink this wine with dessert," says Robert Mazza, who opened his vineyard in 1972 and added ice wine in 1984. "This wine is the dessert."

Growers wait for the grapes to freeze. Then, when they press them, there's less water in the pulp. That makes the sugars stronger.

"It's like drinking liquid gold," says Mazza, whose grapes hint the flavors of peaches, apricots, figs and dates. "It's that sweet and mouth-filling."

It's still a niche business. Mazza bottled just 600 gallons last winter, compared with 6,000 of his top seller, the Niagara table wine. But the market has caught on. For all their other accomplishments, it's ice wine that put Lake Erie growers, and Mazza, on the wine map.

... heard the story of the Mercyhurst College gates.

The posts and scrollwork rise 20 feet, sweeping visitors into an ivied time warp.

The college bought them in 1950. The president then, Mother Borgia Egan, had them shipped from Pittsburgh.

The gates once guarded the estate of Harry K. Thaw, the corrupt son of a Pennsylvania railroad baron. Thaw was a gambler and a scamp, tossed from Harvard for attacking a cab driver. His passion was showgirls - in particular, the exquisite Evelyn Nesbit, whom he met after a performance of "Florodora."

Another suitor beat him to her. Stanford White, the architect of Madison Square Garden, loved Nesbit. Then he left her.

Thaw sought revenge: On June 25, 1906, during a rooftop performance of "Mam'zelle Champagne," he shot White three times.

Thaw was imprisoned, shipped to the Fishkill Correctional Facility in New York. His estate faded. Mother Eagan came for the gates.

Mercyhurst College gates
Nesbit's life inspired a subplot in "Ragtime" and gave shape to "The Girl in the Red Velvet Swing," which starred Joan Collins.

... been in the Whacky Shack.

The classic dark ride, designed by a Macy's window-dresser, is white-knuckle, where's-mom scary - up to a certain age. Then it's just hokey.

The creepy, keep-your-hands-in warning doesn't help. But then the doors bang open, the DayGlo spins you dizzy and the scares start popping out of the dark - A skull! A giant rat! A car, coming right at us!

The ride car bumps and turns and triggers the strobe lights, making the little kids scream. It sounds just like the summer of 1970, when the ride opened, before we needed magnetic brakes, animatronics and a movie tie-in to have fun at an amusement park.

The Whacky Shack
At Waldameer Park & Water World.

... stopped to smell the road-sign flowers.

A dozen have sprung up on Route 322, the road into Meadville.

Their metal petals prep you for the PennDOT fence, a 1,200-foot stretch of remarkable pop-art whimsy. There's a barn made from old stop signs, and a leafy green tree fattened by the markers for Exit 36B. There's a singing cowboy in a NO CROSSING hat and a Ferris wheel that spins three times a day, powered by an old solar highway signboard.

"We wanted to demonstrate to the community the power of art, and the power of re-use," says Amara Geffen, the art professor at Allegheny College who started the sculptures in 2001. "It's fueling a kind of optimism that we can change our community, that we can make it better."

It all comes back to those 10-foot flowers. Their petals are a perfect Adopt-A-Highway blue. And they're always in bloom.

Road-sign art
Route 322, Meadville. Thank the weather for this one: The fence sculpture was envisioned as a living wall, with vines and shrubs. But the road salt killed them off.

... topped off at Fiesler's.

The family-run filling station was built to settle a debt.

The pumps aren't digital yet. There's no touch-screen, five-cheese turkey-melt station, and no Big Gulps to chase it. There's just a dog and a hot pot of free coffee.

It's been that way since 1929, when a man who owed Sam Fiesler some money paid him with cinderblock.

Fiesler did all right for himself. He sold gas to travelers, and for a time he delivered home heating oil. He carried it in 5-gallon buckets.

His grandson runs the place now. He's a tire man. He doesn't hear much fussing from his customers, even with gas at $2.98 a gallon.

His name is Alan Gresh, he says. His business plan is pretty simple.

"It's not about selling stuff," he says. "It's about being good to people."

He smiles, and you remember when they all were called service stations.

Fiesler's gas station
7285 Route 18, Girard. Archie, the dog, was left by a customer. Gresh kept him.

... thanked Ben Franklin for the alatamaha flowers at Goodell Gardens.

The botanist John Bartram and his son discovered this "curious shrub" in Georgia, which they toured in 1765.

The son went back when the plant was seeding, pushing forth gorgeous white flowers. He cut some for his garden in Philadelphia.

The alatamaha thrived there. And that was fortunate, as all the plants that are blooming now - including the 15-foot Goodell shrub, which was planted on Aug. 21, 1962 - came from Bartram's sample. The plant was never again seen in the wild.

Bartram named the shrub for his good friend Benjamin Franklin. The Revolutionary War had started, and Bartram, once the colonial botanist for King George, had picked his side.

The Goodell shrub offers a different kind of sign: A last shot of summer color before the trees turn to skeletons. The alatamaha exits with a grand bow, sprouting 50 flowers a day.

Franklinia alatamaha
At Goodell Gardens and Homestead, 221 Waterford St., Edinboro.

... had a cone of Hank's Frozen Custard.

The go-karts are gone, and the grass has grown over the old track out back. But the creamy treat is still made the same way - in a gravity-fed churn barrel with a beater as long as a boy's leg.

The machines were bought used in 1952, when Henry Grosshans gave his daughter and her husband his recipes for chocolate, butterscotch and peanut butter custard. His one condition: They not open too close to his stand in New Brighton, near Pittsburgh. So they came to Meadville.

They made $4.05 on their first day.

The recipes, heavy in egg yolks and butterfat, have been handed down through two more generations. The custard that comes from it is impossibly soft, and sure to cause a sugar rush, but it says "summer" or "Sunday" or "straight As" better than almost anything.

Hank's Frozen Custard
13940 Conneaut Lake Road, Meadville.

... gawked at the car art parked on Hershey Road.

Some people see faces in clouds. Dick Schaefer sees a bumblebee in the body of a cement mixer.

So he painted one. He put it on legs made from old drive shafts, and he fit a stinger from the fin of a '59 Cadillac.

Then he left it on his lawn, by the dinosaur with spark-plug teeth. They guard his wife's pepper garden.

"Some people love them," Schaefer says of the sculptures. "And some think I'm a wacko."

Some of his quixotic constructions have had consequences: Schaefer twice added on to his garage to cover his ski-shaped boat, a 40-footer he never finished.

Although his first project, a white Lincoln with two front ends, won him a spot in a McKean parade, the ride cost $365.50. A policeman noticed that neither windshield had an inspection sticker.

Schaefer buried half the car in his yard, in a hole he dug by hand. Then he sat in it and laughed.

Dick Schaefer's car art
Hershey Road, west of Peach Street and Route 99.

... clanged the pot sculpture in the West Erie Plaza.

Its five posts are threaded with upturned pots, their bottoms puckered and rusting. A mallet hangs at each end.

The piece is called "Moon Bells." It was built by Barry Miller, a Boston artist. He made another for the Cermak Plaza in Berwyn, Ill. - the home base for David W. Bermant, a developer with an interest in fringe art. Bermant commissioned 28 pieces for the Cermak Plaza, the largest of which - "Big Bil-Bored" - squished 60 tons of car wheels and rusty kitchen appliances into the shape of a three-story pork chop.

Bermant died in 2000. Much of his collection - including a lithograph by Marcel Duchamp - landed at the foundation he began in 1986. But the plaza art has been mostly forgotten. Glass cracked. The pork chop was torn down.

The West Erie Plaza still has a "Good Time Clock," a glass-boxed sculpture animated by a rolling ball. And there's the pots, bolted to the sidewalk by Value City, just waiting for an inspired Salvation Army bell ringer.

... poked around Pithole, the oil town that time tore down.

It was something, once: 57 hotels, three theaters and the third busiest post office in Pennsylvania. The letters home were happy. In 1865, after the Frazier Well came in, plenty of men got rich.

But there were too many wells - even John Wilkes Booth owned part of one - and too many fires. Soon there were too many people: 15,000 living on what had been a farm just nine months before.

The wells dried up, and the dreamers moved on. By 1870, there were just 281 residents left.

These days, especially if it rains, there's often just Fred Sliter, the town's 58-year-old tour guide. He walks the streets, now grown over with grass, and he marvels at how much time can take away.

Pithole Visitor Center
In Venango County. Take Route 8 south to Route 27 east to Route 227 west. Watch for the signs.

... peeked inside the keeper's residence at the Sigsbee Reservoir.

The house, a stick-style Victorian, was home to Sam Pfister, whose job was to watch over 33 million gallons of water. He'd run dogs off the property. He'd row his boat onto the water and take samples. He earned $480 a year.

That was 1875, the height of stick-style, which set planks in geometric patterns, putting an Old World, Swiss Miss twist on a narrow two-bedroom with faded lace curtains.

The west side gets the weather. The olive trim peeled in strips, like sycamore bark. Erie Water Works just fixed it.

They left the interior as it is: empty, with no sign of the two girls who were born there. And that's OK. At Sigsbee, the water is now covered, the work is done by remote and the home, vacant since the 1940s, is only for show.

Sigsbee Reservoir
West 26th St., Erie. The steep banks once were mowed by hungry goats.

... jumped the tabletop at the Scott Park BMX track.

That's Eric Person up in the announcer's tower. He runs the place, dropping the start gate at the Saturday races. His kid is nationally ranked.

The track is at the back of the park, past the ball field and the Rotary trail. There are lights, hot French fries and an arc's worth of fat-tire bikes.

The kids pop off the jumps like caffeinated kangaroos.

"A lot of people are sick of baseball, or sick of soccer," Person says. "This is different. It's a total kid effort. There's no coaches, no captains - just you, mano a mano."

He shouts from the tower, coaxing a 4-year-old through the rhythm section, a dirt washboard that stacks the jumps back-to-back-to back. Then he drops the gate, spurring another batch after her.

Presque Isle BMX
At Scott Park, West Sixth Street, Millcreek.

... thumped a pumpkin at Mason Farms Country Market.

In 1980, when the Mason boys asked their father for a pony, he said OK, as long as they helped pay. So for three days they sold strawberries from the front of their 250-acre Lake City farm. And John Mason saw the promise of roadside produce.

It makes sense, then, that the pumpkin crop now comes with face painting, a corn maze, a haunted house and a hay-bale SpongeBob. And that the front of the market is set up like shop windows, with chicken-wire mannequins topped with painted pumpkin heads. Blues Clues are in there. The "Monsters Inc." crew, too. Because picking a pumpkin should be fun.

The Masons get that - which is why, that first time, they advertised pony rides.

Mason Farms Country Market
839 Peninsula Drive. Leftovers go to the Erie Shriners Hospital for Children and to the Erie Zoo, where the tiger likes to chew.

... taken the train from Union Station.

That was something, once: Rail traffic was so important to the city in the 1850s that a sort of guerrilla war broke out. Rival train lines that had agreed not to match the gauge of their tracks - making Erie a must-stop for all passengers - cut a 4 foot, 10 inch-wide compromise.

City residents fought back, ripping up the track east of Sassafras Street. For months, passengers and freight had to transfer by wagon.

Horace Greeley, the Erie native who edited the New York Tribune, called the dust-up the "Peanut War" because of its effect on local vendors. Even he didn't see the good days ahead, when Union Station opened its showy new space, with a terrazzo floor, Botticino marble and soundproofed rooms for the dispatchers - a novelty in 1927.

More than 700 people still board the Lake Shore Limited every month. For most, though, the station - like the train - is better in memory.

Union Station
Owner Jim Berlin hopes to open a track-side rail museum, featuring Eisenhower's dining car.

... stuffed a dunk at Burton Park.

The nets are worn, and the middle court is missing a backboard, but the games are basketball at its best: blacktopped, trash-talked, city-lot pickup, played fast, for one point a basket, by guys who leave their car keys on the curb.

They play late, under the lights. "You stay on until you've lost," says Mark Sandidge, who waited for the next game.

At Burton, any kid can be Kobe. And an old guy with sore knees can get the one thing we all need: The chance to step up and show our stuff.

Burton Park
East 38th Street and Burton Avenue. The park, once a neighborhood garden plot, also has a tennis camp, a playground and a picnic pavilion.

... walked the planks of the down-rigged U.S. Brig Niagara.

Thick harbor tarps fit the ship like a cocoon, protecting the deck from insensate weather. The carpenters duck under them, getting at the bowsprit, the 40-foot chin of the ship, and the rot that was leaking water in.

The spars are off. The ropes are coiled in a storeroom, the thickest as round as a man's calf.

"This is the engine that runs on air," Senior Capt. Walter Rybka says, stepping through the piles.

The ship is different under cover. The tarps shroud the deck, the one place a sailor can vent the brow-knock claustrophobia below, where the hull narrows and function trumps comfort.

"I suppose it takes some getting used to," Rybka says. "It's kind of like being in the belly of a whale."

The U.S. Brig Niagara
The two-masted flagship, a reproduction of Commodore Oliver Hazard Perry's victory ship at the Battle of Lake Erie, is open for port tours through March.

... wondered how far you are from the Boston Store.

The black-and-white mile-markers first appeared in the 1930s. They were cut from cypress, and then redwood, and then aluminum, and they stood until 1971, when the Highway Beautification Act said they were too close to the roads.

By then they were well known. And the distance had grown. The drive from Rochester, Mich., was 346 miles, according to that sign. From Columbia, S.C., it was 753 miles.

Those signs were ordered by families with Erie ties. For them, the white posts did more than advertise Elisha Mack's once-glorious store. They showed the road home.

Boston Store signs
Mack named his six-floor store for the Massachusetts capital, which was then a center of fashion and culture. His original sales staff - just eight clerks - had to grow into the role: On market days, they helped farmers sell produce on the sidewalk.

... sought solace in the spring color at the Erie Cemetery.

The buds are out now. The boughs of the crabapples are heavy with petals. They reach over what would have been Walnut Street, back in May of 1851, when workers dug the first of 50,000 graves, and they form a canopy the color of wine spilled on a white shirt.

Walk there, and you'll wrestle the big questions. Sit in the pergola, with its high white gothic columns, and you'll see the leavings of grief - new tulips, a puckered Mother's Day balloon, a flag for the old Army sergeant.

Close your eyes, and consider the time we have here, and you'll hear birds, and the noon church bells, and the putter of lawn mowers, which is the sound of a remembrance tended.

Erie Cemetery
2116 Chestnut St. Open every day from 8 a.m. until dusk.

... tried to spy home from the top of the Bicentennial Tower.

Sure, it's touristy, stuffing quarters into those buy-the-minute viewfinders. But the day looks different at 187 feet.

The city seems greener, past Hamot Medical Center and the Boston Store clock and the onion domes of the Old Orthodox Church of the Nativity. The boats below, lined up for the channel, for a day in the lake that buried the Samana, the Groten and the Anthony Wayne, look small, like pieces from a train-set town. But the water is bluer than you ever remember.

On a clear day, it goes all the way to Canada. It reminds you why you live here.

Bicentennial Tower
The $2.1 million tower, open since 1995, has become a hot spot for marriage proposals. The staff has hosted a few of the weddings as well.